I0478038

Digital Marketing Mastery for Small Business Success

Chapter 1: Introduction to Digital Marketing

Understanding Digital Marketing

Digital marketing encompasses a range of strategies and tools designed to promote products and services through the internet. For real estate investors and small business owners, mastering digital marketing is not merely advantageous; it is essential for staying competitive in an increasingly online marketplace. Unlike traditional marketing, digital marketing allows for targeted outreach, enabling businesses to connect with specific demographics. This targeted approach results in more efficient use of marketing budgets and higher conversion rates, as businesses can tailor their messages based on audience behaviors and preferences.

Social media marketing is a critical component of digital marketing that can significantly benefit small businesses. Platforms like Facebook, Instagram, and LinkedIn offer unique opportunities for engagement and brand building. Real estate investors can showcase properties through visually compelling posts, while small business owners can share customer testimonials and behind-the-scenes content that humanizes their brand. Leveraging social media allows businesses to interact directly with potential customers, fostering relationships that can lead to increased loyalty and sales.

Content marketing is another vital strategy within the digital marketing landscape, especially for e-commerce brands. Creating valuable, relevant content not only helps in attracting customers but also establishes authority and trust within the industry. For small businesses, regularly updated blogs, videos, and infographics can drive traffic to their websites and enhance their SEO efforts. By focusing on high-quality content that addresses customer pain points and interests, businesses can improve their online visibility and encourage organic growth through search engines.

Search Engine Optimization (SEO) is an essential practice for local businesses aiming to increase their online presence. SEO involves optimizing website content and structure to rank higher in search engine results, thus driving more organic traffic. Local SEO strategies, such as incorporating location-based keywords and optimizing Google My Business listings, are particularly effective for businesses serving specific geographic areas. This practice ensures that potential customers can easily find relevant services and products when searching online, making it a crucial tactic for small businesses looking to thrive in local markets.

Influencer marketing and data analytics are two additional facets of digital marketing that can enhance campaign effectiveness. Collaborating with influencers allows businesses to reach wider audiences through trusted voices in their niches, making it easier to promote niche products. Meanwhile, data analytics provides insights into customer behavior and campaign performance, enabling businesses to refine their strategies for optimal results. By leveraging these tools, small business owners can not only increase their market reach but also make informed decisions that drive long-term success in the competitive digital landscape.

Importance for Small Businesses

Digital marketing has become an essential component for small businesses, particularly in competitive fields such as real estate investment, e-commerce, and local services. Unlike traditional marketing methods, which often come with high costs and uncertain returns, digital marketing offers a more accessible and measurable approach. For small business owners, this means the ability to reach a broader audience without the need for a substantial budget. By leveraging various digital channels, businesses can create targeted campaigns that resonate with their specific customer base, ultimately driving growth and success.

Social media marketing stands out as a particularly powerful tool for small businesses, enabling them to engage directly with their audience. Platforms like Facebook, Instagram, and LinkedIn provide an opportunity for real estate investors and entrepreneurs to showcase their offerings, share valuable content, and foster relationships with potential customers. By implementing effective social media strategies, businesses can not only increase their visibility but also build a community around their brand, which is crucial for long-term loyalty and engagement.

Content marketing is another vital aspect for small businesses, especially in e-commerce and niche markets. By creating high-quality, valuable content that addresses the needs and interests of their target audience, businesses can establish themselves as industry authorities. This approach not only enhances brand credibility but also improves search engine rankings, driving organic traffic to websites. For small businesses, content marketing can be a cost-effective way to attract and convert leads, ultimately leading to increased sales and customer retention.

Search engine optimization (SEO) is critical for local businesses looking to improve their online presence. By optimizing their websites for relevant keywords and ensuring they are listed on local directories, small businesses can enhance their visibility in search engine results. This is particularly important for real estate investors and service providers who rely on local clientele. Implementing SEO best practices can lead to higher website traffic, increased leads, and improved conversion rates, allowing small businesses to compete more effectively in their respective markets.

Finally, data analytics plays a crucial role in optimizing digital marketing campaigns for small businesses. By analyzing customer behavior, engagement metrics, and conversion rates, businesses can make informed decisions about their marketing strategies. This data-driven approach allows small business owners to identify what works and what doesn't, enabling them to allocate resources more efficiently and refine their tactics over time. For nonprofits and other organizations, understanding their audience through analytics can significantly enhance fundraising efforts and community engagement initiatives, ultimately leading to greater impact and success.

Overview of Key Strategies

In the dynamic landscape of digital marketing, small businesses, including real estate investors and e-commerce brands, must adopt key strategies to enhance their online presence and drive success. Understanding the core components of digital marketing can empower these businesses to leverage various channels effectively. This overview focuses on essential strategies such as social media marketing, content creation, search engine optimization, influencer engagement, and data analytics. By integrating these tactics, small businesses can create a robust marketing framework that yields measurable results.

Social media marketing has emerged as a vital tool for small businesses to engage with their target audience. Platforms like Facebook, Instagram, and LinkedIn offer unique opportunities for real estate investors and small business owners to showcase their products and services. By developing a consistent posting schedule, utilizing targeted advertising, and engaging with followers through comments and direct messages, businesses can build a loyal community and increase brand awareness. Additionally, creating shareable content can amplify reach and foster organic growth, making social media an indispensable component of any digital marketing strategy.

Content marketing plays a crucial role in establishing authority and trust within a niche. For e-commerce brands and small businesses, producing high-quality, relevant content not only attracts potential customers but also enhances search engine rankings. Blog posts, videos, and infographics can educate the audience about products and services, while also addressing their pain points. A well-defined content calendar that aligns with the overall marketing objectives can help maintain consistency. This strategic approach to content creation not only drives traffic but also nurtures leads through informative and engaging material.

Search engine optimization (SEO) is essential for local businesses aiming to increase visibility in search results. Implementing best practices such as keyword research, on-page optimization, and local listings can significantly improve a business's online presence. For small businesses, focusing on local SEO tactics like Google My Business optimization and acquiring local backlinks can help attract nearby customers. By understanding the importance of local search behavior, businesses can effectively position themselves in front of potential clients searching for their services in the vicinity.

Influencer marketing is another effective strategy for small businesses looking to reach niche markets. Collaborating with influencers who resonate with their target audience can enhance credibility and drive sales. Identifying the right influencers, establishing mutually beneficial partnerships, and creating authentic content can amplify a brand's message significantly. Additionally, measuring the impact of these collaborations through engagement metrics and sales conversions helps refine future influencer marketing efforts, ensuring that resources are allocated effectively.

Data analytics serves as the backbone for optimizing marketing campaigns. By analyzing user behavior, conversion rates, and campaign performance, small business owners can gain insights into what strategies work best for their audience. Tools such as Google Analytics and social media insights provide valuable data that can inform decision-making. By continuously monitoring and adjusting marketing efforts based on analytical findings, businesses can maximize their return on investment, ensuring that their digital marketing strategies evolve in line with changing consumer preferences and market trends.

Chapter 2: Using Digital Marketing Effectively

Creating a Digital Marketing Plan

Creating a digital marketing plan is essential for real estate investors, small business owners, internet marketers, and those working from home to navigate the complexities of the digital landscape. A well-structured plan provides clarity and direction, ensuring that marketing efforts align with business goals. Start by defining your objectives, which could range from increasing brand awareness to generating leads or improving customer retention. Clear goals will serve as the foundation for your strategy and will guide your choice of tactics and channels.

Once your objectives are established, it is crucial to identify your target audience. Understanding who your customers are will help tailor your marketing messages and select the right platforms for outreach. Create detailed buyer personas that include demographics, interests, pain points, and buying behaviors. This information will enable you to develop content that resonates with your audience and meets their specific needs, whether you are promoting real estate listings or e-commerce products.

Next, consider the various digital marketing channels available to you. Each channel, such as social media, email marketing, SEO, and content marketing, offers unique advantages. For instance, social media platforms are great for engaging with audiences and building community, while SEO can enhance your visibility in search engine results, driving organic traffic to your website. Assess the strengths of each channel in relation to your target audience and objectives, and choose a combination that maximizes your reach and effectiveness.

Content creation is a fundamental component of your digital marketing plan. High-quality, relevant content not only drives traffic but also establishes your authority in your niche. Invest time in developing a content calendar that outlines your topics, formats, and distribution strategies. Whether you are creating blog posts, videos, or social media updates, ensure that your content is valuable and aligns with your audience's interests. This approach will foster engagement and encourage sharing, amplifying your marketing efforts.

Finally, implementing data analytics is critical for monitoring the performance of your digital marketing plan. Utilize tools that track key performance indicators (KPIs), such as website traffic, conversion rates, and social media engagement. Regularly analyze this data to identify trends, successes, and areas for improvement. By adjusting your strategies based on data insights, you can optimize your campaigns for better results, ultimately leading to greater success in your digital marketing endeavors.

Setting Measurable Goals

Setting measurable goals is a crucial step in any digital marketing strategy, particularly for real estate investors, small business owners, and internet marketers. The process begins with defining

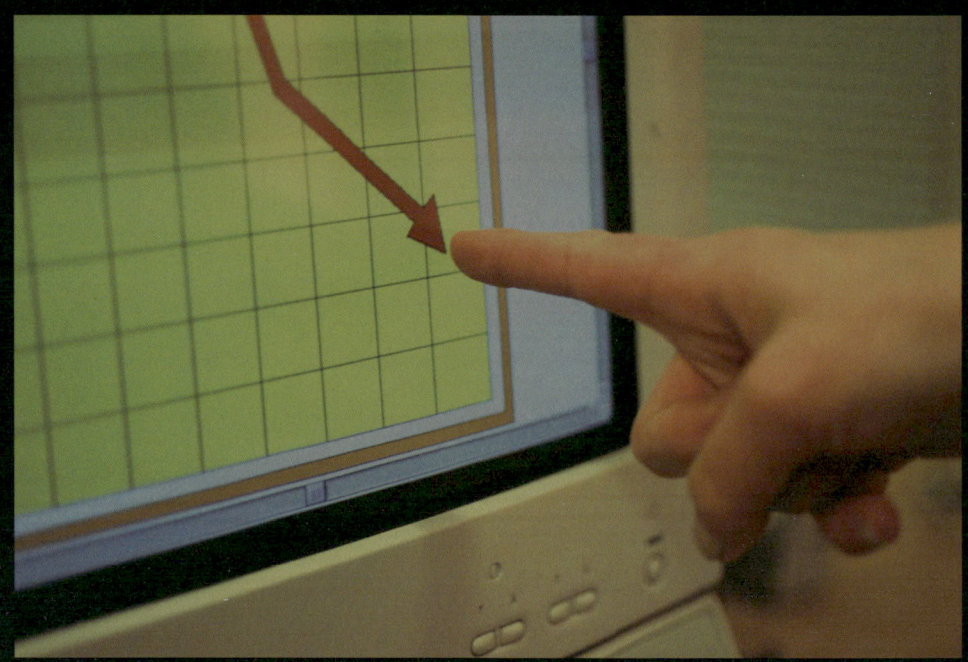

ISBN 9798344803036

9 798344 803036

90000